Elias Hill
101 So Bad, They're Good Dad Jokes
Copyright 2017
Self-published, Tiny Camel Books

Tiny Camel Books
tinycamelbooks.com
tinycamelbooks@gmail.com

101
So Bad,
They're Good
Dad
Jokes

By: Elias Hill

Illustrations By: Katherine Hogan

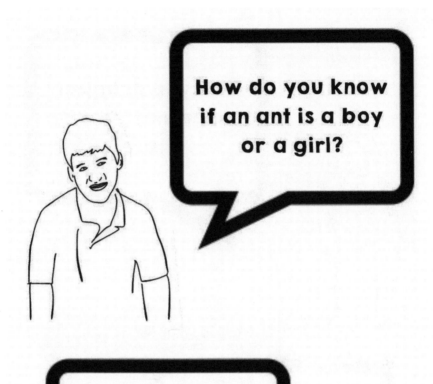

Dad, you dropped a pea off your plate.

Oh my, looks like I've pea-ed on the table.

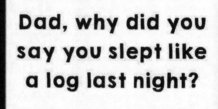

Dad, why did you say you slept like a log last night?

Because I woke up in the fireplace.

Dad, how do stop a bear from charging?

Take away his credit cards.

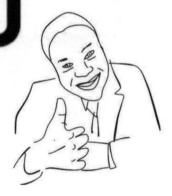

Dad, Mrs. Lee offered me a job babysitting and doing light housework.

But you don't know anything about lighthouses!

Dad if you could have any superpower in the world what would it be?

China.

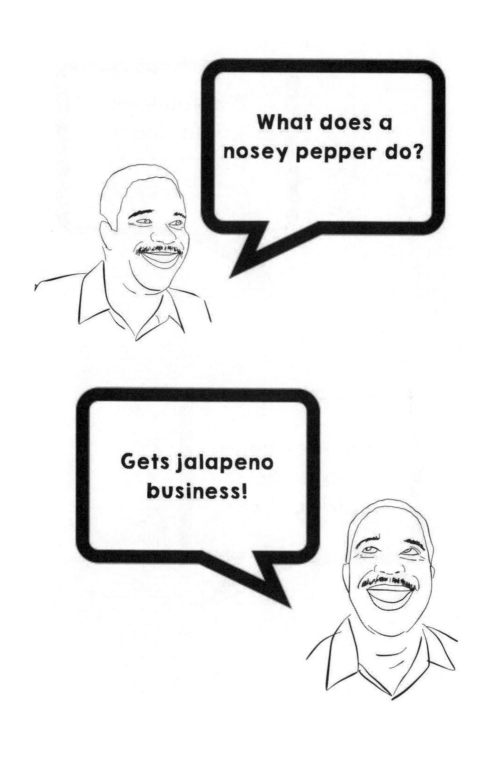

Did you hear koala bears aren't really bears?

Yep, they don't have the koalafications.

Dad, I'm having an allergic reaction, we need to get to a hospital!

Well, let's not make any rash decision.

Dad, what's the difference between a numerator and a denominator?

A short line. Only a fraction of people understand that.

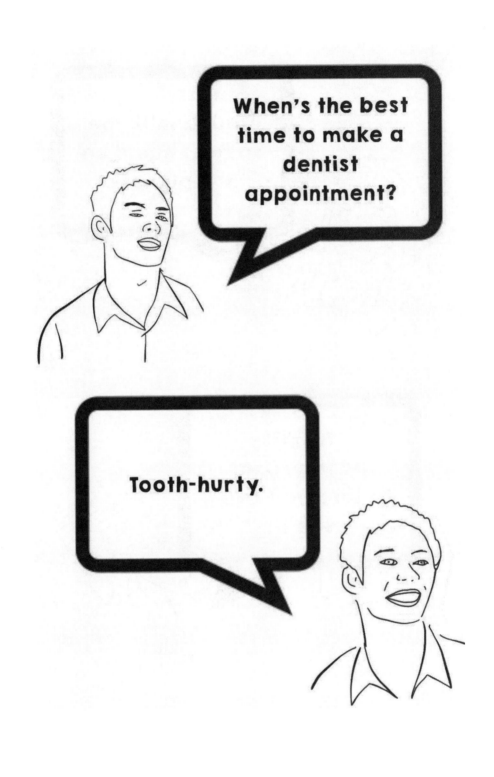

Enjoy this book?

We would really appreciate a review on Amazon!

Be sure to check out our other dad jokes books as well.

Join our Readers' Club and hear about new releases and receive previews before our books are released!

http://bit.do/tinycamel